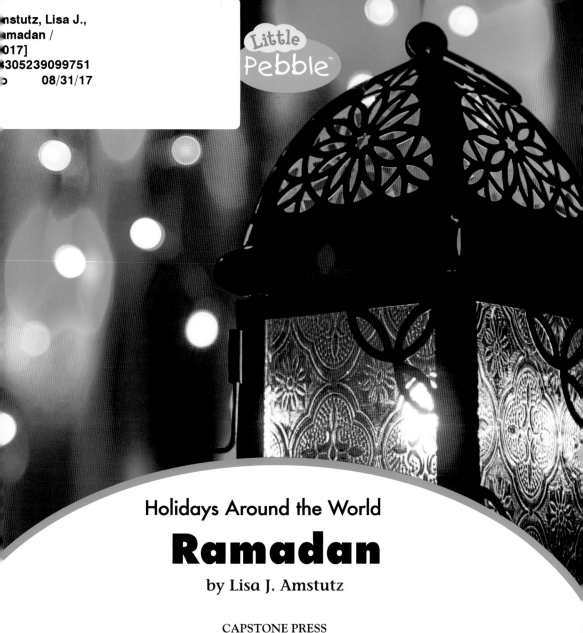

Little Pebble™

Holidays Around the World

Ramadan

by Lisa J. Amstutz

CAPSTONE PRESS
a capstone imprint

Little Pebble is published by Capstone Press,
1710 Roe Crest Drive, North Mankato, Minnesota 56003
www.mycapstone.com

Library of Congress Cataloging-in-Publication Data
Names: Amstutz, Lisa J., author.
Title: Ramadan / by Lisa J. Amstutz.
Description: North Mankato, Minnesota : Capstone Press, [2017] | Series: Little
    pebble. Holidays around the world. | Includes bibliographical references and index.
Identifiers: LCCN 2016034425 | ISBN 9781515748564 (library binding) |
    ISBN 9781515748625 (paperback) | ISBN 9781515748809 (eBook (pdf))
Subjects: LCSH: Ramadan—Juvenile literature. | Fasts and feasts—Islam—
    Juvenile literature.
Classification: LCC BP186.4 .A6 2017 | DDC 297.3/62—dc23
LC record available at https://lccn.loc.gov/2016034425

Editorial Credits
Jill Kalz, editor; Julie Peters, designer; Pam Mitsakos, media researcher;
Steve Walker, production specialist

Photo Credits
Getty Images: Rich-Joseph Facun, 17; iStockphoto: SoumenNath, 5; Shutterstock: Aisylu
Ahmadieva, 11, AmazeinDesign, 15, callmerobin, 1, 22, 24, back cover, clicksahead,
cover, Digital Saint, design element, Firas Nashed, 10, JOAT, 3, Kertu, 13, MidoSemsem,
21, Mrs_ya, 9, muratart, 19, rSnapshotPhotos, 6 inset, ZouZou, 7, 14

Printed and bound in China.
PO7884LEOS17

Table of Contents

What Is It?

Be kind to one another.

Ramadan is here!

Ramadan is a time to be good. It lasts one month.

Time to Pray

People do not eat
all day. They do not
drink either.

People pray.

They think about God.

People do kind things.

They help others.

They give food and money.

The sun sets.

People light candles.

They eat dates.

Then they eat a meal.

Time for Joy

The month is over.

Families have a feast.

They thank God.

Pop! Boom!

Fireworks fill the sky.

The party lasts three days.

It is a happy time.

Glossary

date—a kind of fruit

feast—a large, fancy meal for a lot of people on a special occasion

fireworks—rockets that make loud noises and colorful lights when they explode

pray—to speak to God and give thanks

Ramadan—a Muslim holiday; Muslims follow the religion of Islam

Read More

Bullard, Lisa. *Rashad's Ramadan and Eid al-Fitr.*
Minneapolis: Millbrook Press, 2012.

Khan, Hena. *Golden Domes and Silver Lanterns: A Muslim
Book of Colors.* San Francisco: Chronicle Books, 2012.

Whitman, Sylvia. *Under the Ramadan Moon.* New York:
AV2 by Weigl, 2013.

Internet Sites

FactHound offers a safe, fun way to find Internet sites
related to this book. All of the sites on FactHound have
been researched by our staff.

Here's all you do:
Visit *www.facthound.com*
Type in this code: 9781515748564

Critical Thinking Using the Common Core

1. Name three things people may do during Ramadan. (Key Ideas and Details)

2. At the end of Ramadan, families have a feast. What is a feast? (Craft and Structure)

Index